Mad about...

Ponies

written by Sandy Ransford
illustrated by Ian Escott

A catalogue record for this book is available from the British Library

Published by Ladybird Books Ltd
80 Strand London WC2R 0RL
A Penguin Company

2 4 6 8 10 9 7 5 3 1
© LADYBIRD BOOKS LTD MMVIII
LADYBIRD and the device of a Ladybird are trademarks of Ladybird Books Ltd

ISBN-13: 9781 84646 800 1

Printed in China

Contents

Some words appear in **bold** in this book.
Turn to the glossary to learn about them.

A pony's life

Ponies in the wild live in family groups called herds. The herd is made up of a male pony (the stallic a number of female ponies (mares) and their foals. A pony is called a foal until it is one year old. Ponie are not fully grown until they are four or five years old. They may liv until they are twenty-five to thirty years old or more.

Ponies spend most of their time eating grass.

Young foals drink
their mothers' milk.

If something frightens the ponies,
the herd can gallop away very fast.

7

Ponies and people

Ponies first lived on Earth about 65 million years ago. They were very different then. People began to keep ponies about 6,000 years ago, using them for pulling **chariots** in battles and for hunting wild animals. Later, ponies were ridden. For thousands of years, **horses** and ponies were the only form of transport on land.

The earliest pony was the size of a fox and had toes on its feet.

The Romans
used ponies for
chariot racing.

Strong, heavy horses
were used for farm
work. Before there
were machines to
help, horses pulled
carts and ploughs.

Ladies rode
side-saddle until
recent times.

9

Points of a pony

The points of a horse or pony are the parts of its body that you can see. The difference between horses and ponies is that a horse is 14.3 **hands high** or taller, and a pony is up to 14.2 hands high.

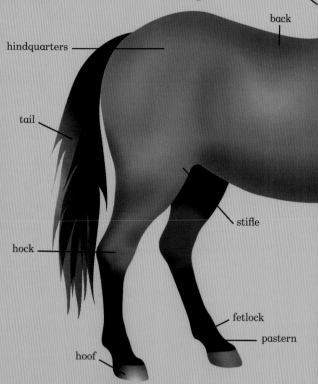

withers

back

hindquarters

tail

stifle

hock

fetlock

pastern

hoof

mane

forelock

neck

cheek

muzzle

shoulder

knee

There are many different types and **breeds** of horses and ponies. Here are two of the biggest and smallest.

Shetland pony   Shire horse

If you have a computer, you can download a poster of different breeds from www.ladybird.com/madabout

Colours and markings

Most ponies are brown, but each shade of brown has a different nam

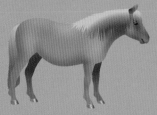

Chestnut ponies are a reddish-gold colour all over.

Bays are a red-brown colour w a black mane, tail and lower l

Brown ponies are dark brown with black manes and tails.

Piebald ponies have black and white patches all over.

Greys are dark or **dappled** when young and white when they get older.

Palominos are gold-coloured with a white mane and tail.

Ponies often have white markings on their faces and legs.

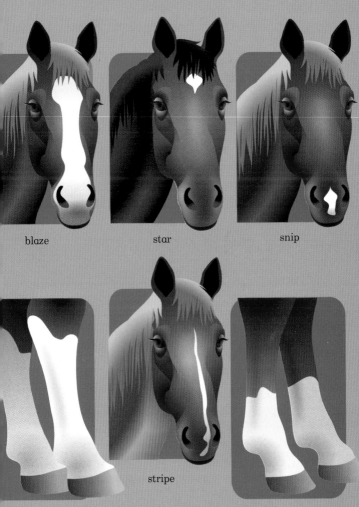

blaze

star

snip

stripe

stockings

socks

Where to keep a pony

You can keep a pony in a stable or a field. Many ponies spend half their time in the stable, and half out in the field. That way they get some shelter from the weather, and some freedom to graze and roam around.

A stable must be big enough for a pony to move about. Ponies need lots of fresh air, so the top half of the door should always be open.

A pony's field must be properly fenced. It needs a clean water supply and some sort of shelter. This can be thick hedges, shady trees or a **field shelter.**

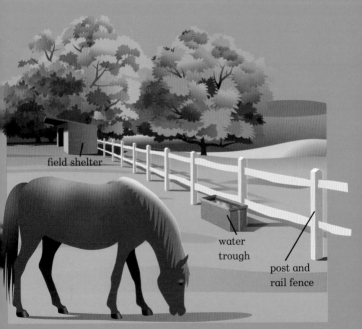

field shelter

water trough

post and rail fence

15

Handling a pony

Ponies are large, strong animals, but they are easy to handle. They like people to be quiet, calm and friendly. If you shout or rush about, it makes them nervous.

Meeting a pony
Speak to a pony in a friendly way and give it a pat on the neck.

In the stable
To get a pony
to move in
its stable,
push on its
hindquarters
and say,
"Get over."

Leading a pony
You lead a pony on
its left-hand side.
Hold the rope in
both hands. Your
right hand should
be near its head and
your left hand on
the end of the rope.

17

Pony care

Ponies need a lot of looking after. They must be fed and groomed, and their stables cleaned out. They should always have fresh water near by. Even if they live in a field they need checking twice a day.

Feeding

In summer, ponies can live on grass. In winter, they need hay as well. They also need hay if they are kept in a stable. If they work hard, they need extra food, too

18

Mucking out

Droppings and wet bedding must be cleaned out of the stable every day.

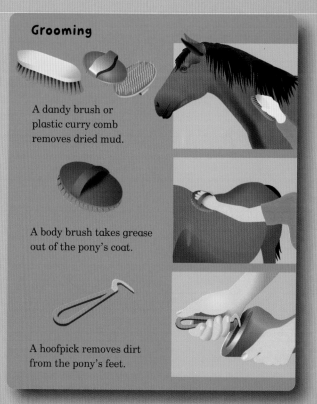

Grooming

A dandy brush or plastic curry comb removes dried mud.

A body brush takes grease out of the pony's coat.

A hoofpick removes dirt from the pony's feet.

Shoeing a pony

Ponies wear iron shoes to stop their hooves wearing down. But the hooves grow, like your nails, so every six to eight weeks the shoes must be taken off and the pony's feet trimmed. This is done by a **farrier**

1 First the farrier cuts the nail ends, called clenches, that hold the shoe on the foot. He pulls off the shoe with pincers.

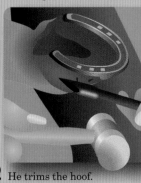

2 He trims the hoof. Then he **rasps** the surface smooth.

3 He heats the shoe in a furnace, then hammers it into shape on an **anvil**.

4 He tries the hot shoe on the pony's foot. It burns the hoof, making a lot of smoke, but the pony cannot feel it.

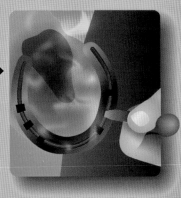

5 He cools the shoe in a bucket of cold water, then nails it on to the pony's foot.

The nails come out of the side of the hoof. The farrier twists off ends of the nails, then hammers them down to form the clenches.

7 With the pony's foot resting on a tripod, the farrier rasps the hoof and clenches smooth.

21

A pony's tack

A pony's saddle, bridle, and other equipment it wears when it is ridden, is called **tack**. It is usually made of leather. Tack needs cleaning with **saddle soap** to keep it in good condition.

Snaffle bridle

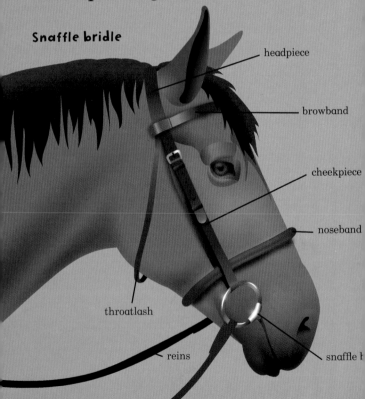

headpiece

browband

cheekpiece

noseband

throatlash

reins

snaffle b

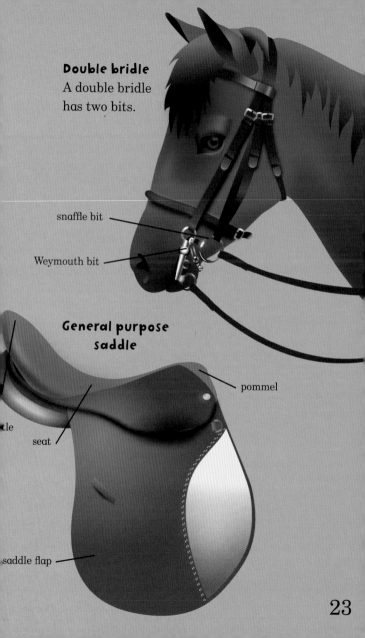

Double bridle
A double bridle
has two bits.

snaffle bit

Weymouth bit

General purpose saddle

pommel

tle

seat

saddle flap

23

Riding clothes

When you ride a pony, you must wear a hard hat. **Jodhpurs** and boots are more comfortable than ordinary clothes.

To protect your head you need a riding hat or a skull cap. A skull cap may be covered by a colourful silk.

For jumping, you need a body protector to stop you hurting your back if you fall off.

On your feet you can wear long riding boots or jodhpur boots. Long boots stop the stirrup leathers pinching your legs.

Riding gloves have rubber pimples on the palms so that you can hold the reins in wet weather.

A riding
hat has a
hard brim

You can
wear a smart
**hacking
jacket** or
a casual one

Jodhpurs stop your
legs getting rubbed

25

A pony's paces

Ponies have four natural **paces**, or ways in which they move forwards: walk, trot, canter and gallop. The walk is the slowest and the gallop the fastest.

Walk
You sit down in the saddle when a pony walks.

rot

When a pony trots
its feet hit the
ground in diagonal
pairs: left front and
right hind, right
front and left hind.
You rise out of the
saddle for one beat
and sit for the other.

Canter

In the canter, the
front and hind leg
on one side are in
front of those on
the other. This is
called the leading leg.

Gallop

When you gallop,
you raise yourself
out of the saddle
and lean slightly
forwards.

27

Riding activities

There are lots of ways you can enjoy riding. Going out for a ride in the countryside is called hacking. You may ride in an enclosed area, called a school, to improve your pony's paces and learn to jump. You could join a local riding club, and compete in events such as show jumping and **gymkhanas**

Dressage needs a very well-schooled pony or horse.

The cross-country part of **eventing** involves galloping and jumping.

In a potato race, you have to pick up a potato, gallop down the field, and put it in a bucket – all from your pony's back.

Glossary

anvil – a heavy metal block on which hot horseshoes are hammered into shape.

breeds – groups of horses and ponies with features in common.

chariot – a small, horse-drawn carriage.

dapple – light and dark hairs that form rings of colour on a pony's coat.

dressage – advanced training of a ridden horse or pony.

eventing – a competition consisting of dressage, a cross-country course with jumps, and show jumping.

farrier – someone who shoes a horse or pony.

field shelter – a large open-fronted shed in a field.

gymkhana – an event with games and races performed on horseback.

hacking jacket – a smart wool jacket worn for riding.

hands high – horses and ponies are said to be so many "hands high". A hand is ten centimetres or four inches.

horse – an animal over 14.2 hands high (147 centimetres).

jodhpurs – riding trousers with extra layers on the insides of the legs to stop rubbing from the saddle.

pace – the way a horse or pony moves its legs at different speeds.

pony – an animal up to and including 14.2 hands high (147 centimetres).

rasp – a file used to smooth rough edges on a pony's hoof when it is being shod.

saddle soap – a special kind of soap that softens leather, used for cleaning tack.

tack – the saddle, bridle and other equipment used on a riding pony.